Cars, Cars, Cars

Michael Steer

Contents

Changing the World

Cars have changed our world. They have changed how we live.

This car was made in 1896.

This car was made in 2008.

Cars have also changed how we get to places.

Long ago, people used carts to get from place to place.

New Cars Every Year

In 2009, over 50 million new cars were made around the world!

First Cars

The first car used **steam** to make it go. It was very slow. It was built over 200 years ago.

The First Car Crash

This first steam car crashed into a wall. This was the first car crash ever!

The first **petrol** car was made around 120 years ago. Today, most cars use petrol to make them go.

Most people could walk faster than the first petrol car!

In the early 1900s, not many people had a car. Cars cost a lot of money and most people could not buy them.

Only rich people could buy the first cars.

An American man called Henry Ford wanted everyone to be able to buy a car. So, he started making them! Cars were made quickly and **cheaply** at his **factory**.

Henry Ford driving the first car he built

The Model T Ford was made in Henry Ford's factory around 100 years ago.

Cars and More Cars

By 1912, hundreds of cars were being made each day. Today, thousands and thousands of cars are made each day!

Today, robots help to make cars in car factories.

Shaping Up

Over the years, cars have changed shape a lot. The first cars looked nice but they could not go fast. Today, cars can look good and go fast too!

a 1926 Morris Oxford

a Lamborghini Murcielago

Cars Everywhere!

Cars changed how people lived. People drove to places instead of walking to them. They drove to work and school. They even drove their cars on holidays.

a 1960s car and caravan

People even went to see movies and stayed in their cars!

a drive-in movie

Just Drive In!

Today, you can wash your car and buy food without getting out of your car. You can even go to the bank!

All Kinds of Cars

Today, there are many kinds of cars. There are:

4-wheel-drive cars

mini cars

funny-looking cars

racing cars

family cars

A Car or a Boat?

This car can drive on the road and float on the water. It can even go under the water like a submarine!

Problems with Cars

There are over 600 million cars in the world. All these cars use a lot of petrol. Using a lot of petrol is bad for Earth.

The amount of petrol used in America each day would fill 600 big swimming pools!

Big Problem 1

Cars need petrol to go. But the petrol in the engines makes smoke. This smoke is called **air pollution.** It can make people and animals sick.

Big Problem 2

Petrol is made from oil. Oil is made under the ground – it takes millions of years. Once oil runs out, petrol will run out. How will cars go if there is no petrol?

No Petrol!

Today, some new cars use less petrol or no petrol at all! They use other things to make them go.

These cars use **electricity** and petrol to make them go.

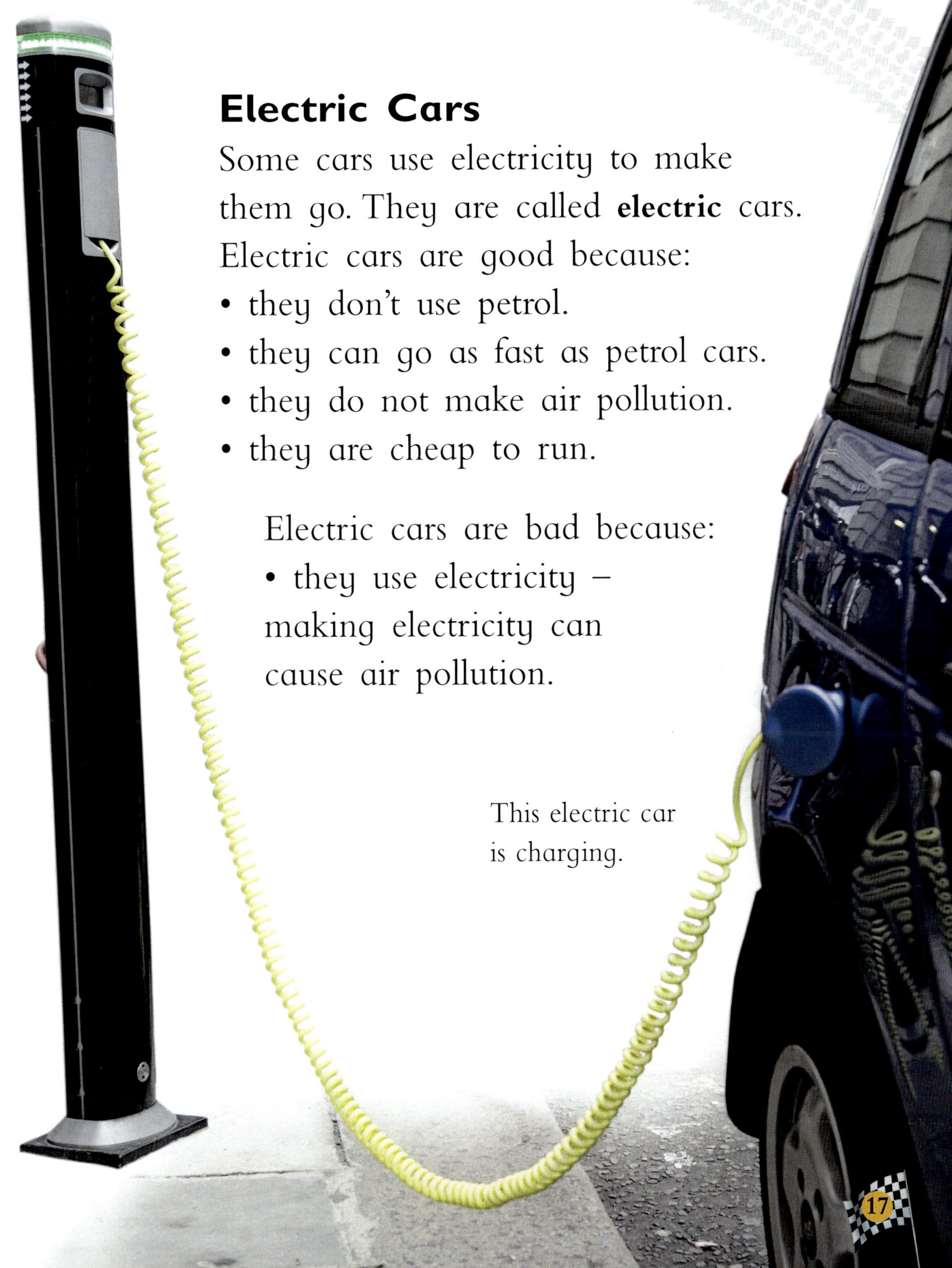

Electric Cars

Some cars use electricity to make them go. They are called **electric** cars.

Electric cars are good because:

- they don't use petrol.
- they can go as fast as petrol cars.
- they do not make air pollution.
- they are cheap to run.

Electric cars are bad because:

- they use electricity – making electricity can cause air pollution.

This electric car is charging.

Solar Cars

Some cars use **energy** from the sun to make them go. They are called **solar** cars. Solar cars are good because:

- they do not use petrol.
- they do not make air pollution.
- they are cheap to run.

a solar racing car

Solar cars are bad because:

- they go very slowly.
- they use **batteries** – making batteries can cause air pollution.

The First Solar Car

The first solar car was made in 1955. It was called the Sun-mobile!

Fast Cars

Some cars are made to go very, very fast. They can travel almost as fast as a jet plane. **Wow!**

a Formula One racing car

How Fast?

a racing car — over 360 km an hour

a car today — 225 km an hour

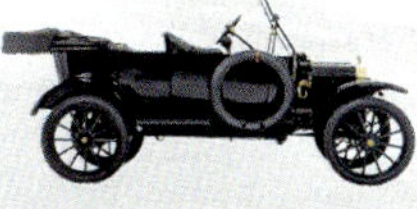

the Model T-Ford — 72 km an hour

a person walking — 6.5 km an hour

That's Fast!

This is one of the fastest cars in the world today. It can travel at around 400 kilometres an hour!

Cars Are Stars!

Cars come in many shapes, sizes and colours.

Cars with Funny Names

Have you heard of these funny car names?

- the Mini
- the Beetle
- Dragster
- Go-Go Mobile
- Chitty Chitty Bang Bang?

Who knows what cars will be like in the future? Maybe you will get in your car and fly away!

Glossary

air pollution
smoke that goes into the air and is bad for you and the planet

batteries
items that hold electricity

cheaply
not costing a lot

electric
getting energy from electricity

electricity
an electric power or current

energy
a kind of power, like solar power or electricity

factory
a place where something is made

petrol
a kind of fuel used in some engines to make them go

solar
getting energy from the sun

steam
the mist in the air made from boiling water